Cape Cod Critters

©Brian Tague Photography

Written & Illustrated by Lorri Devlin

Published in the USA by Little Minnow Press

P.O. Box 232, Mashpee, MA 02649

ISBN 978-0-615-46257-8

Cape Cod

life is everywhere-
in ponds and forests, lakes and air.

Some critters live beneath the sand.
Some you can fit right in your hand.
Some live up high in tree top nests.
Some think that salty water's best.

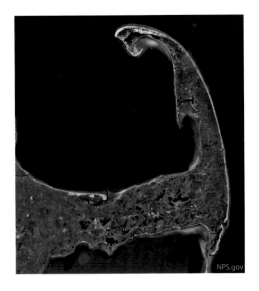

Some are giant; some so small that they are barely seen at all.

Are you ready to explore ? Let's turn the pages to learn more.

The shy Box turtle builds its house with leaves and meadow grass.

NPS.gov/Brad Timm

Turkey families stroll along the roads and country paths

U.S. Wildlife Fisheries Service

The Spadefoot Toad hides underground
and waits for summer rain.

When Cape Cod nights turn wet and
warm, he'll venture out again.

Two stealthy night-time hunters are Coyote and the Owl.

You'll know they've caught some dinner if you hear a HOOT and HOWL.

Barred Owls

Eastern Coyote

The Osprey dives with talons wide to grab a fish up quick.

His family waits for breakfast
in a nest made out of sticks.

Clams live under tidal flats.
Walk over them-they'll squirt you.

Jellyfish are squishy.
Stay away-their sting can hurt you.

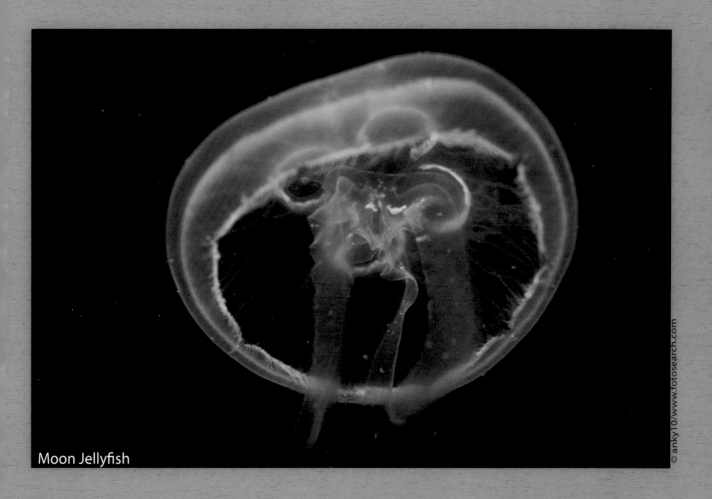

Moon Jellyfish

Stripers chase the shiny lures of fishermen with poles.

Striped Bass

NOAA.gov

ed-tailed hawks hunt berry bogs for jumping mice and moles.

uh-oh!

Hermit crabs have shells that look like periwinkle snails

©Devlin

Lobsters have antennae.

NOAA.gov

Horseshoe crabs have pointy tails.

The Herring is a little fish that swims from stream to sea

NOAA.gov

How does it know which way to go ?
It is a mystery.

L.D

Piping plover parents build their nests in shoreline sand.

Brian Tague Photography

When baby chicks are hatching, no one walks on plover land.

A **Mako shark** is small, but it can swim as fast as lightning

NOAA.gov/Mark Conlin

Bluefish have sharp teeth like sharks,
but they are not as frightening.

Starfish will grow back a foot if one of theirs goes missing

Flounders have a funny face that isn't good for kissing.

A baby fox is called a kit.

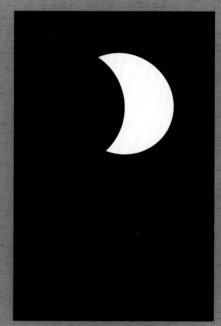

Brian Tague Photography

Red foxes wake at night.

NPS.gov

Baby fish are spawn or fry... so either word is right.

Atlantic Cod's the fish that gave Cape Cod
its name, for sure...

Greetings from Cape Cod

Greetings from
Cape Gadus Morhua

If we had used its Latin name, we'd be Cape Gadus Morhu

lever Seagulls drop their seashells 'til they open wide.

Herring Gull

David Harrington

ey race their friends down to the ground to eat the food inside.

White-tailed deer roam on Cape Cod
from Bourne right down to Chatham.

National Park Service

This is a baby Harbor seal.

You'll smile when you look at him.

Stellwagen Bank's a place where tiny plankton can be fo

NOAA.gov

Brian Tague Photogra

Every day a Humpback whale can eat 4,000 pounds!

Visit These Places To Learn More About Cape Cod Critters.

Happy Exploring!

©Devlin

Cape Cod Museum of Natural History, Brewster, MA
www.ccmnh.org

Greenbriar Nature Center, East Sandwich, MA
www.thorntonburgess.org

Long Pasture Wildlife Sanctuary, Barnstable, MA
Wellfleet Bay Wildlife Sanctuary, South Welfleet, MA
www.massaudubon.org

Woods Hole Science Aquarium, Woods Hole, MA
aquarium.nefsc.noaa.gov

Cape Critters Rock!

NOAA: Robert Cook

Photo: WHOI

Visit: www.capecodcritters.net

About the Author

Lorri Devlin, BSN, MS, RN

Lorri Devlin spent childhood summers playing outside in the
abundant natural beauty of Cape Cod. She believes that creating a
life-long bond with nature brings physical, emotional and spiritual benefits
to children, and encourages respect for natural resources.
She can be reached at lorridevlin@gmail.com.

The National Park Service/Cape Cod National Seashore reminds visitors
to remain on trails and boardwalks; do not approach or touch wildlife;
and follow park rules designed for visitor safety and resource protection.

With special thanks to Steve Devlin, Sue Moynihan,
National Park Service/Cape Cod National Seashore, NOAA, U.S. Wildlife Fisheries Service,
Leslie Hatton, Woods Hole Oceanographic Institute,
& my ancestors, who taught me to tread softly upon this precious planet.

Ask
PRINTING & PUBLISHING SERVICES
Paul Petrie (617)-816-8903